ASSATEAGUE
Island of the Wild Ponies

Andrea Jauck & Larry Points

MACMILLAN PUBLISHING COMPANY   •   NEW YORK

MAXWELL MACMILLAN CANADA   •   TORONTO

MAXWELL MACMILLAN INTERNATIONAL
NEW YORK   •   OXFORD   •   SINGAPORE   •   SYDNEY

Assateague is an American Indian word thought to mean
"the marshy place across."

The authors wish to express gratitude to friends who contributed photos,
and in particular to Dr. Ronald Keiper, whose research provides the
basis for much of what is known about Assateague Island's wild ponies.

Photo credits: National Park Service (NPS), pages 1, 4 (top), 7 (top), 8 (top), 13 (bottom), 22, 23 (bottom), 28, 29 (bottom); Douglas Buehler, page 3; Terry Bashore, pages 4 (bottom), 11, 30 (top); NPS/Harvey Wickwire, page 5; NPS/Mitch Fong, pages 6 (top), 9; Rick Naugle, page 6 (bottom); Ronald Keiper, pages 7 (bottom), 8 (bottom), 10, 15 (bottom), 16 (top), 17, 21 (bottom), 24 (top right); Larry Points, pages 12, 24 (top left), 29 (top left), 32; William Perry, page 13 (top); Roger Clapp, page 14; NPS/Carol McNulty, page 15 (top); U.S. Fish and Wildlife Service, pages 16 (top), 26; NPS/ Richard Frear, page 18; NPS/Len McKenzie, page 19 (top); Jerry Via, page 19 (middle); Lisa Ludvico, pages 19 (bottom), 21 (top); Debbie Burley, page 20; NPS/Gordon Noreau, page 23 (top); Beverly Points, page 24 (bottom); Jeff Chynoweth, page 25; NPS/Allison Turner, page 27; William Perry, page 24 (top); Jay Kirkpatrick, page 30 (bottom); Gary Ludwig, page 31.
The map on page 32 is based on materials provided by the National Park Service; we gratefully acknowledge their help.

Macmillan Publishing Company is part of the Maxwell Communication Group of Companies.
Macmillan Publishing Company, 866 Third Avenue, New York, NY 10022
Maxwell Macmillan Canada, Inc., 1200 Eglinton Avenue East, Suite 200, Don Mills, Ontario M3C 3N1
First edition
Printed in the United States of America

10 9 8 7 6 5 4 3 2 1

The text of this book is set in 14 point Palatino. Book design by Constance Ftera.
Library of Congress Cataloging-in-Publication Data
Jauck, Andrea.
Assateague : island of the wild ponies / by Andrea Jauck and Larry Points. — 1st ed.
p.   cm.
Summary: Describes the life and natural environment of the wild ponies that live on the
long barrier island off the Maryland and Virginia coast.
ISBN 0-02-774695-X
1. Chincoteague pony—Assateague Island (Md. and Va.)—Juvenile literature.   2. Natural
history—Assateague Island (Md. and Va.)—Juvenile literature.   3. Assateague Island (Md.
and Va.)—Description and travel—Juvenile literature.   [1. Chincoteague
pony. 2. Ponies. 3. Assateague Island (Md. and Va.)] I. Points,
Larry. II. Title.
SF315.2.C4J38   1993   599.72′5—dc20   92-5908

To the children of Assateague and their joy of discovery

Springtime returns to Assateague Island. The cold winter is gone. Now warm, salty breezes blow across the beach. Delicate heather blooms on the dry, sandy dunes. Blue crabs wake from their long sleep in the bay's soft mud. Birds sing as they build new nests in the forests and marshes. Everywhere the island is bustling with activity as animals prepare to raise new families. Spring is the time when babies are born on Assateague.

Assateague is a long barrier island off the coasts of Maryland and Virginia. On one side is the Atlantic Ocean; on the other, a calm bay. The island is home to many animals, both large and small. The larger animals are mammals like deer, raccoons, and red fox. Assateague's biggest mammal is also the island's most famous resident.

Wild ponies are the most famous animals on Assateague Island. Like other island animals, most of the ponies have their babies, or foals, in the spring. The mother, or mare, is pregnant a long time—almost a year.

When she is ready to give birth—usually at night—the mare wanders away from other ponies. She finds a quiet place near bushes or sand dunes where nothing will frighten the foal. After the foal is born, the mother licks and smells it so she will be able to find it among all the other foals.

Foals can walk a few minutes after they are born, though their legs are still wobbly. Soon they run and play, exploring their island world. Foals are very curious about all the strange new things around them, yet they are careful not to wander too far from their mothers.

The frisky foals are always hungry and they spend a lot of time nursing. A newborn foal nurses five times each hour, both day and night, while its mother stands patiently. Foals begin to nibble grass a few weeks after birth, but they still need their mothers' warm, rich milk for several months.

Foals quickly learn to recognize the other ponies in their family group, or band. Each band is made up of a strong male horse called a stallion, several mares, and their young. The stallion is the leader of the band. He tries to protect the ponies from any danger, such as contact with people or other stallions. Some bands are small, with only three or four ponies. Other bands have as many as twelve ponies. Ponies in the same band stay close together. They communicate by making different kinds of sounds, and by sniffing each other and rubbing noses.

Ponies often imitate each other. If one pony yawns when it is sleepy, soon the ponies nearby are yawning, too.

Sometimes a stallion will walk with his ears pulled back and his neck stretched low, waving his head from side to side. This action is called snaking. It tells the band that danger may be near and that they should start to run. The band gallops off, with the stallion close behind. He may nip mares with his teeth if they don't run fast enough.

Stallions often try to add to their bands by stealing mares from each other. A stallion may have to fight to protect his band. When stallions fight, they rear up on their back legs and try to hit or bite one another. Each pony tries to show the other he is stronger. Stallions and mares can also kick out with their powerful hind legs when they become angry.

Sometimes a stallion will start a fight with his older son, or colt. This is a signal that it is time for the young pony to leave the band before he challenges the stallion for control. Small groups of colts wander the island in "bachelor herds." Soon they become strong enough to attract young females, or fillies, and each young stallion starts his own band.

Foals practice fighting when they are in their family groups and later as bachelor colts. This is how they learn the skills needed to defend their bands when they grow up.

Most of the time, ponies look for food in different island areas called habitats. One of the ponies' favorite habitats is the wet, muddy salt marsh, which is a grassy meadow that is partly covered with salt water during high tides. A band will stay for hours in a marsh eating the coarse, salty grass that grows there. This grass is very tough to chew, so ponies have to grind it with their teeth a long time.

The salt marsh is very important to many other animals. Wading birds, snails, mussels, and crabs feed and live among the wet grasses. Tiny pieces of decaying grass end up in the bay and are eaten by fish, clams, and shrimp. Some scientists think that the salt marsh food chain may help feed most of the creatures in the northern Atlantic Ocean.

The odd-looking fiddler crab spends its whole life in the salt marsh. The male has one very large claw that he waves around to attract female crabs.

A shallow bay lies between Assateague's salt marshes and the mainland. Shrubs and trees on the island protect the bay from ocean storms. Many fish and other sea animals come to these quiet waters to have their young. Lots of birds also live on or use the bay.

Healthy salt marshes and bays like the ones here are becoming rare. Many marshes have been filled in so that buildings could be put on them. The quality of the water is bad in many places. A lot of people are working hard to keep Assateague Island and its surrounding waters free of pollution.

Young skates (fish shaped like a stingray) hatch from black egg cases in the bay. They share the bay habitat with many other sea creatures, including the horseshoe crab. The gentle horseshoe is not a true crab—it is more closely related to the spider. Horseshoe crabs are ancient creatures; they were walking on the ocean bottom when dinosaurs roamed the earth.

Ponies need the bay, too. Sometimes a pony band will wade out into the cool water on hot, buggy days. They are careful not to walk in too deep—hungry foals still have to nurse.

Ponies need to drink a lot of water after eating salty marsh grass. Sometimes they sip a little salt water, but they usually drink fresh water from small island pools and ponds. Many ponds are found in the loblolly pine forest, which is another Assateague habitat. Tall trees shelter these ponds from salt and sand carried in the wind.

Ponds are also a good place to see wildlife. Sika deer, opossums, and other animals come here to drink. Many birds like to nest near ponds, too.

It is shady and peaceful under the pines. After the ponies take a long drink, they may take a nap. Foals lie down in the pine needles to sleep. Some adults do, too, but most "lock" their knees and sleep standing up; some even sleep with their eyes open.

After resting for about an hour, the ponies are hungry again. They eat the berries and leaves of many forest plants, even poison ivy. Most people get an itchy rash from this abundant island plant, but it does not seem to bother the ponies.

Many people come to the island to see birds as well as ponies. The great blue heron is one of Assateague's largest birds, and a very good hunter. The heron can grab fish, crabs, turtles, and even snakes with its long, sharp bill.

Busy little sandpipers run up and down the beach. They dart between waves, looking for tiny pieces of food in the sand.

Piping plovers lay their eggs right in the sand. The mother bird sits on the eggs and chicks to protect them from the hot sun.

The cattle egret has a special relationship with the ponies. It eats insects off their coats and gets a free ride in return. A patient pony will even let a cattle egret pick insects from between its eyes.

Summer is the hardest season for the ponies. It is often very hot and sticky. Biting flies and mosquitoes can force the ponies out of the marsh or forest, onto the beach.

If there are too many insects on the beach, the ponies may wade into the ocean and let waves crash over their backs.

Rolling on the ground is another way to get rid of pesky bugs. Ponies swish their tails in each other's faces, rub themselves on bushes, and run, shaking their manes. They'll do anything they can to get away from insects.

Ponies often run to a high sand dune, where ocean breezes keep biting pests away. They spend a lot of time in the sand dune habitat eating the beach and dune grasses that grow there. Sand dunes are much like a hot, dry desert where only special plants and animals can live.

American beach grass is a very important plant in the sand dune habitat. It has long roots that grow deep into a dune in search of fresh water. These roots help hold the sand together when strong winds or waves strike the dune.

The hognose snake is a common resident of the sand dunes. Though harmless to people, it is a predator that hunts and eats other animals, especially toads. Ponies are not hunted by predators on Assateague, but there is one source of danger....

People can be a hazard to ponies. Some visitors feed the ponies unhealthy foods; this draws the ponies to roads where some may be hit, injured, or even killed, by cars. Ponies can be dangerous to people, too. They might look tame and friendly, but they really are wild animals. They can kick or bite without warning. A pony might even tear a camper's tent to reach food it sees or smells.

Island rangers spend a lot of time talking to people about the ponies. Visitors can watch the ponies eat and play—but only from a safe distance.

Some rangers and scientists study the ponies to learn more about them. They may patiently follow a band for hours to see how the ponies behave.

Scientists have discovered that most ponies live to be about twenty years old. Life is harsher on the island than on a farm, where domestic horses can live thirty or more years.

Since the Assateague ponies are only a little smaller than the average horse, researchers do not consider them to be a true pony breed. Real ponies, like the Shetland, are quite small in comparison. However, Assateague's horses have always been called "ponies" by people living around the island, and by adoring children everywhere.

There are two main herds of ponies on Assateague. The Maryland ponies on the north end of the island are managed by the National Park Service. The Virginia ponies, on the south end, are owned by the volunteer fire company from nearby Chincoteague Island. The Virginia ponies are rounded up the last week of July each year in a famous event called Pony Penning. Fire fighters on horseback search the dunes and marshes to round up all the pony bands. They shout and crack their long whips to keep the ponies together.

The fire fighters drive the ponies into the bay. The ponies then swim across a narrow channel to Chincoteague Island while thousands of people watch and cheer. The next day, many of the foals are sold in an auction to raise money for the fire company. Foals are easy to tame and usually make gentle pets. Some very happy boys and girls leave Chincoteague with new friends.

Soon all the other ponies swim back to Assateague. They quickly form into bands and resume their island life for another year. Pony roundups have been taking place for over one hundred years. But ponies have not always been on Assateague Island. How did they get there?

Some people think that the ponies came ashore from a ship that sank in a storm, but no one knows for sure. Researchers do know that mainland farmers brought horses to barrier islands about three hundred years ago to let them graze. Some of these horses could not be found by their owners and became wild.

Shipwrecks still occur at Assateague during storms. Powerful hurricanes can strike the island in late summer and autumn. In other seasons there are strong ocean storms called northeasters. Waves crash over the dunes and the wind howls. Sand blows everywhere. The ponies hide deep in the forest until the storm is over.

Autumn can also be a very calm, beautiful season. Biting insects and the summer crowds of tourists disappear. Hundreds of monarch butterflies flutter through the dunes and feed on goldenrod blossoms as they migrate south. The air is filled with the wild calls of snow geese as they, too, journey south.

Assateague is often still and silent in winter. Most of the birds have flown south. Even some fish have migrated to warmer waters. Other animals, like crabs and snakes, hibernate, sleeping through the long winter months. The lonely beach has few visitors now. The wind is cold and damp. But winter can be beautiful, too. A rare snowfall turns the island into a white fairyland.

In winter, ponies grow thick, shaggy coats to protect them from the cold. Although winter can be harsh, the ponies can still find enough dried grass to eat. Ponies actually have an easier life in the winter than they do during the hot, buggy summer.

The winter days pass slowly, but spring brings new life again. Soon another generation of foals will play in the warm sun and discover the wonders of life on Assateague Island.

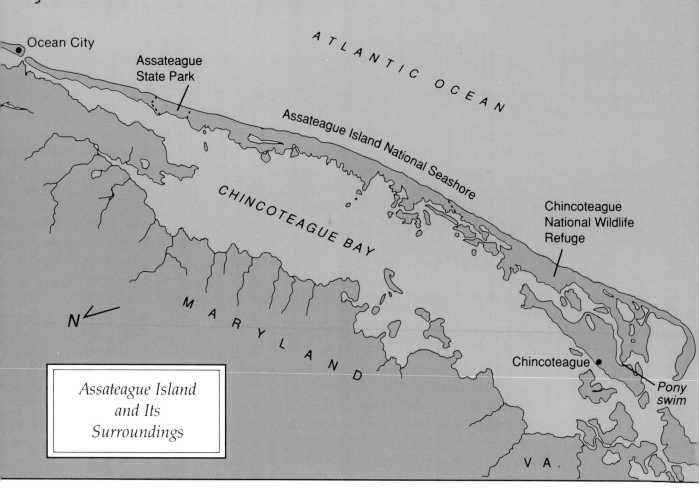

Assateague Island
and Its
Surroundings

Wild ponies and Assateague Island. The two have been inseparable since colonial times. National interest first came in 1948 with the publication of *Misty of Chincoteague*. Assateague became a national seashore in 1965. Located 120 miles east of Washington D.C., the island is easily accessible to visitors.

Twin forces of wind and wave subject sandy barrier islands to constant change. Assateague is no exception, and its natural beauty was rearranged in January, 1992 by the greatest storm to strike the shore in thirty years. These photos, taken from the same spot before and after the storm, bear witness. Waves flattened the dunes and carried in heavy black sand from offshore bars.

To learn more about nature and recreational opportunities write to: Assateague Island National Seashore, 7206 National Seashore Lane, Berlin, MD 21811.